Watching Stars

by Tracy Stanley

Watching Stars copyright 2020 by Tracy Stanley
all rights reserved. No part of this publication may be reproduced or
transmitted in any form or by any means, including photocopy, record-
ing, or any information storage and retrieval system,
without permission in writing from the publisher
Angels and Architects
ISBN 978-0-578-67048-5

this book is dedicated
to
my niece emelia joy hall
and
my nephew ezra joseph hall

Do you like to

watch stars at night?

Have you ever seen

a shooting star ?

How many shooting

stars have you seen?

Did you make a wish

on a star?

Do the stars move

or sparkle?

What color

are stars ?

Do you like to

draw stars ?

Will you look out of your car window,

to watch some stars tomorrow?

Can you be friends

with a star?

Maybe you will watch

some stars tonight?

www.ingramcontent.com/pod-product-compliance
Lightning Source LLC
Chambersburg PA
CBHW041412160426

42811CB00107B/1771

9780578670485